HIGHER MUSIC PRACTICE PAPERS

Graeme Brownlee & John Montgomery

To access the online Higher music exams please go to

www.softplanetgroup.com/highermusic

PAPER A............................... 2

PAPER B............................... 14

PAPER C............................... 26

PAPER D............................... 38

PAPER E............................... 52

Copying of this book is strictly forbidden. Please contact us at the address below if you need any further information on licensing, sales or content.
SOFTPLANET LTD
Greenbank House, Prior Muir, St Andrews, KY16 8LP. 01334 461244
hq@softplanetgroup.com www.softplanetgroup.com

ISBN 978-0-9934657-0-3

IMPORTANT NOTE
This book is not Licensed for school/college use.
Please go to our website to order a School Licence Pack

PAPER A

QUESTION 1

This question features instrumental music.
Listen to this excerpt and identify **three** concepts in the music from those listed below.

Read through the concepts before hearing the music.

Harmonic minor scale	Sequence	Harmonics
Swing Rhythm	Polyphonic	Rallentando
Concerto grosso	Oboe	Classical

Insert your **three answers** on the lines below.   3

_____

_____

_____

The music will be played **twice** with a pause of 10 seconds between playings and a pause of 40 seconds before the next question starts.

Here is the music for the first time.
Here is the music for the second time.

QUESTION 2

In this question you will hear a vocal soloist accompanied by orchestra.

A guide to the music is shown below. You are required to complete this guide by inserting music concepts.

There will now be a pause of 30 seconds to allow you to read through the question.

The music will be played **three** times with a pause of 20 seconds between playings. You will then have a further 30 seconds to complete your answer.

In the first two playings a voice will help guide you through the music. There is no voice in the third playing.

Here is the music for the first time.
Here is the music for the second time.
Here is the music for the third time.

1. The Woodwind instrument playing the melody is a/an

   _____ 1

2. The male vocal soloist is a/an

   _____ 1

3. The cadence is

   _____ 1

4. The upper strings are playing

   _____ ⎫
                                       ⎬ 1
   The lower strings are playing   ⎭

   _____

5. The word setting at this point is

   _____ 1

QUESTION 3

This question features contrasting music for voices.

(a) Listen to this excerpt and insert the concept which describes the style of the music.

_____

1

(b) Listen to a different excerpt and insert the name of the concept which describes the type of modulation.

_____

1

(c) Listen to a different excerpt and identify the final cadence.

_____

1

PAPER A

QUESTION 4

Marks

This question is based on a vocal composition.

Listen to the song and follow the guide to the music on the next page.

Here is the music for the first time.

You now have 2 minutes to read the question.

All the answers must be written where indicated on the next page.

(a) Identify the **key** the music is in at **bar 1.** 1

(b) Describe the interval formed by the two notes in **bar 6**. 1

(c) Add rests to the music in **bar 13** to make the bar correct. 1

(d) Insert the missing notes in bar **15 and 16.** The correct rhythm is written above these bars. 1

(e) Insert the missing bar lines in the second last line (from **bar 19**) 1

(f) Insert the chords you hear in the last line. You may use letter names or numbers. The first 2 chords are given. 1

Choose from the following:

D   Chord I
G   Chord IV
A   Chord V
Bm Chord VI

Insert your answers in the boxes provided.

During the next three playings complete your answers (a) to (f).
The music will be played **three** more times with a pause of 30 seconds between playings and a pause of 2 minutes before the next question starts.

Here is the extract for the second time
Here is the extract for the third time.
Here is the extract for the last time

PAPER A

QUESTION 5

This question features instrumental music.

(a) Listen to this excerpt and tick **one** box to describe the rhythmic feature.

☐ Compound time

☐ Diminution

☐ 3 against 2

☐ Augmentation

1

(b) Listen to a different excerpt and identify the concept which describes the texture of the brass chords.

_____

1

(c) Listen to a further excerpt from the same work and identify the final cadence.

_____

1

Additional space for notes

(Turn over for Question 6)

QUESTION 6

This question is based on instrumental music.

In this question you should identify the most prominent concepts in the music.
As you listen, identify at least **two** concepts from each of the following headings:

Melody/Harmony   **Rhythm**   **Texture**

You will hear the music **three times** and you should make notes as you listen.

Rough work will not be marked.

Marks will only be awarded for the final answer.

After the third playing you will have 3 minutes to write your final answer in the space provided.

Here is the music for the first time.
Here is the music for the second time.
Here is the music for the third time.   **6**

Rough Work

Melody/Harmony	
Rhythm	
Texture	

Final Answer

PAPER A

QUESTION 7

This question features music for vocal soloists, choir and instrumental accompaniment.

Listen to this excerpt and identify **four** concepts in the music from those listed below.

Read through the list before hearing the music.

Time changes	Mass
Modulation	Lied
Da capo aria	Interrupted cadence
Pentatonic	Syllabic
Augmentation	Coloratura

Insert your **four** answers on the lines below.   4

_____

_____

_____

_____

The music will be played **three** times with a pause of 10 seconds between playings and a pause of 40 seconds before the next question starts.

Here is the music for the first time.
Here is the music for the second time.
Here is the music for the third time.

QUESTION 8

This question is about comparing two excerpts of music.

Identify concepts present in each excerpt and then decide which **five** concepts are common to both excerpts. Both excerpts will be played **three** times with a pause of 10 seconds between playings.

As you listen, tick boxes in **Column A** and **Column B** to identify what you hear in Excerpt 1 and Excerpt 2.

These columns are for rough work only and will not be marked.

PAPER A

After the **three** playings of the music you will be given 2 minutes to decide which concepts are common to both excerpts and to tick **five** boxes in **Column C**.
You now have 1 minute to read through the question.

Here is Excerpt 1 for the first time. **Remember to tick concepts in Column A.**
Here is Excerpt 2 for the first time. **Remember to tick concepts in Column B.**

Here is Excerpt 1 for the second time.
Here is Excerpt 2 for the second time.

Here is Excerpt 1 for the third time.
Here is Excerpt 2 for the third time.

You now have two minutes to identify the **five** concepts common to both excerpts.
Remember to tick five boxes only in Column C.   5

	Concepts	Column A Excerpt 1	Column B Excerpt 2	Column C 5 features common to both
Melody/Harmony	Imitation			
	Dominant 7th			
	Pedal			
	Mordent			
Rhythm	Rallentando			
	Irregular time signature			
	3 against 2			
Timbre	Harmonics			
	Tremolo			
	Ripieno			
Structure/Form	Basso continuo			
	Contrary motion			
	Ternary			

QUESTION 9

This question is based on a song from a musical.

Below is a list of features which occur in the music.

There will now be a pause of 1 minute to allow you to read through the question.

The lyrics of the song are printed in the table on the opposite page. You should insert each feature **once** in the column on the right at the point where it occurs.

You need only insert the underlined word.
- **Diminished 7th** chord
- First line in which a **Pedal** point starts
- First phrase with **no anacrusis**
- **Perfect** cadence
- Descending **chromatic** phrase in bass

The music will now be played **three** times with a pause of 20 seconds between playings and a pause of 30 seconds at the end.

Here is the music for the first time.
Here is the music for the second time.
Here is the music for the third time.

- **Diminished 7th** chord
- First line in which a **Pedal** point starts
- First phrase with **no anacrusis**
- **Perfect** cadence
- Descending **chromatic** phrase in bass

Insert the **five** underlined words at the point they occur. 5

Insert each word once only.

See the big parade on the esplanade	1
And the firework display.	2
There's the juggler's hoops	3
And the dancing troupes	4
Working the night and day.	5
If you want to stay for the matinee	6
Don't worry you can't go wrong.	7
Relax, sit down find a place on the ground	8
For the show it must go on.	9
Come buy a ticket	10
To the greatest show in town	11
See the latest and the	12
Greatest under lights.	13
Come buy a ticket	14
It's the greatest show around	15
Have the best time of your life	16
With us tonight.	17

End of question paper

PAPER B

QUESTION 1

This question features instrumental music.
Listen to this excerpt and identify **three** concepts in the music from those listed below.

Read through the concepts before hearing the music.

Imitation	Tierce de Picardie
Basso continuo	Plagal cadence
Irregular time signatures	Cross rhythms
Cadenza	Impressionism
Passacaglia	

Insert your **three answers** on the lines below.   3

_____

_____

_____

The music will be played **twice** with a pause of 10 seconds between playings and a pause of 30 seconds before the next question starts.

Here is the music for the first time.
Here is the music for the second time.

QUESTION 2

In this question you will hear instrumental music.

A guide to the music is shown below. You are required to complete this guide by inserting music concepts.

There will now be a pause of 30 seconds to allow you to read through the question.

The music will be played three times with a pause of 20 seconds between playings. You will then have a further 30 seconds to complete your answer.

In the first two playings a voice will help guide you through the music. There is no voice in the third playing.

Here is the music for the first time.
Here is the music for the second time.
Here is the music for the third time.

---

1. The time signature is

   _____   **1**

2. The cadence is

   _____   **1**

3. The chord outlined is

   _____   **1**

4. The melody and bass lines are playing in

   _____   **1**

5. The music has modulated to

   _____   **1**

QUESTION 3

This question features contrasting music for voices.

(a) Insert the concept which
 (i) describes this type of work and
 (ii) describes the texture of the voices.

 (i)_____
                                     1

 (ii)_____
                                     1

(b) Listen to a different excerpt and name the vocal style.

   _____
                                     1

QUESTION 4

This question is based on a song from a musical.

Listen to the song and follow the guide to the music on the next page.

Here is the music for the first time.

All the answers must be written where marked on the next page.

(a) Write the correct <u>note names</u> on the line provided above **bar 3**. 1

(b) Insert the <u>rest</u> in **bar 5** to make this bar correct. 1

(c) Add an <u>accidental</u> in **bar 7** to match what you hear. 1

(d) Insert the <u>notes</u> in **bars 9, 10 and the first beat of 11** to match what you hear. The correct rhythm is written above. 1

(e) Add <u>bar lines</u> from **bar 13** to the end of the second last line. 1

(f) Add the names of 3 <u>chords</u> you hear in the last line (**bars 18-20**) The first chord is given. You may use letter names or numbers. The first chord is given.

Choose from the following:
You can choose the chord name (eg; C) or the chord position (eg; chord I)

C   Chord I

F   Chord IV

G   Chord V

Am   Chord VI 1

Complete your answers during the next three playings.

The music will be played 3 more times with a pause of 30 seconds between playings.

Here is the music for the second time
Here is the music for the third time
Here is the music for the fourth time

PAPER B

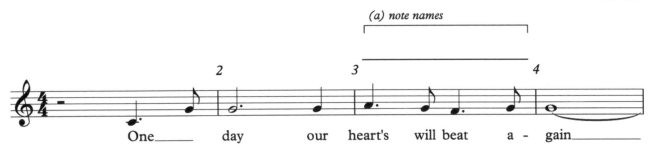
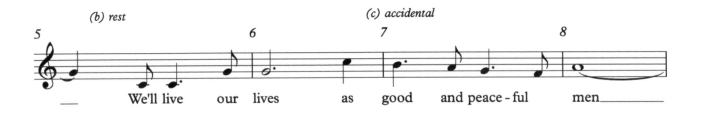
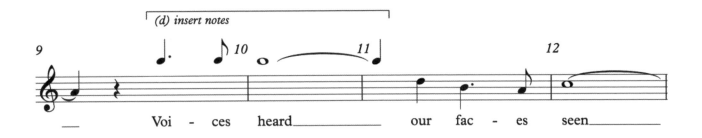
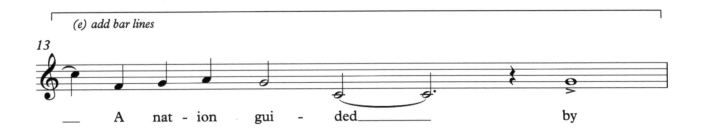
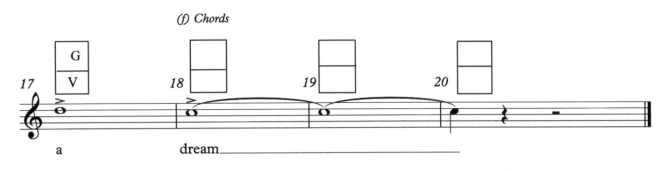

17

PAPER B

QUESTION 5

This question features instrumental music.

(a) Listen to this excerpt and tick **one** box to describe the rhythmic feature.

☐ 3 against 2

☐ Augmentation

☐ Diminution

☐ Irregular time signatures

Here is the music for the first time.   **1**
Here is the music for the second time.

(b) Listen to the following excerpt and insert the concept which describes the style of the music.

_____
                                                                                                   1

(c) Listen to a different excerpt. Insert the concept which describes the style of the music.

_____
                                                                                                   1

PAPER B

Additional space for notes

(Turn over for Question 6)

PAPER B

QUESTION 6

This question is based on instrumental music.

In this question you should identify the most prominent concepts in the music.
As you listen, identify at least **two** concepts from each of the following headings:

Melody/Harmony   **Rhythm**   **Timbre**

You will hear the music **three times** and you should make notes as you listen.

Rough work will not be marked.

Marks will only be awarded for the final answer.

After the third playing you will have 3 minutes to write your final answer in the space provided.

Here is the music for the first time.
Here is the music for the second time.
Here is the music for the third time.   **6**

Rough Work

Melody/Harmony	
Rhythm	
Timbre	

20

Final Answer

PAPER B

QUESTION 7

This question features vocal music.

Listen to this excerpt and identify four concepts in the music from those listed below.

Read through the list before hearing the music.

Through composed	Anacrusis
Tenor	Oratorio
Lied	Mode
Plainchant	Diminished 7th
Imperfect cadence	Ritornello

Insert your four answers on the lines below.   **4**

_____
_____
_____
_____

The music will be played **three** times with a pause of 10 seconds between playings and a pause of 40 seconds before the next question starts.

Here is the music for the first time.
Here is the music for the second time.
Here is the music for the third time.

QUESTION 8

This question is about comparing two excerpts of music.

Identify concepts present in each excerpt and then decide which **five** concepts are common to both excerpts. Both excerpts will be played **three** times with a pause of 10 seconds between playings.

As you listen, tick boxes in **Column A** and **Column B** to identify what you hear in Excerpt 1 and Excerpt 2.

These columns are for rough work only and will not be marked.

After the **three** playings of the music you will be given 2 minutes to decide which concepts are common to both excerpts and to tick **five** boxes in **Column C**.

PAPER B

You now have 1 minute to read through the question.

Here is Excerpt 1 for the first time. **Remember to tick concepts in Column A.**
Here is Excerpt 2 for the first time. **Remember to tick concepts in Column B.**

Here is Excerpt 1 for the second time.
Here is Excerpt 2 for the second time.

Here is Excerpt 1 for the third time.
Here is Excerpt 2 for the third time.

You now have two minutes to identify the **five** concepts common to both excerpts.
Remember to tick five boxes only in Column C.

5

	Concepts	Column A Excerpt 1	Column B Excerpt 2	Column C 5 features common to both
Styles	Concerto			
	Sonata			
	Classical			
	Romantic			
Melody/Harmony	Imitation			
	Sequence			
	Modulation to relative minor			
	Pedal			
Rhythm	Augmentation			
	Simple time			
	Rubato			
Timbre	Harmonics			
	Pizzicato			
	Tambourine			

PAPER B

QUESTION 9

This question is based on a contemporary song.

Below is a list of features which you will hear in the music.

There will now be a pause of 1 minute to allow you to read through the question.

The lyrics of the song are printed on the next page. You should insert each feature you hear once in the right column at the point it occurs.

You need only write the underlined word.

- Ascending **scale** in strings
- **Tierce** di picardie
- **Ostinato**
- Inverted **pedal**
- **Tremolo**

The music will now be played three times with a pause of 20 seconds between playings, and a pause of 30 secs at the end.

Here is the music for the first time.

Here is the music for the second time.

Here is the music for the third time.

- Ascending **scale** in strings

- **Tierce** di picardie

- **Ostinato**

- Inverted **pedal**

- **Tremolo**

It's getting late now	1
Pretty colours in the sky.	2
You're laughing on a bus	3
And you really don't know why.	4
Nothin's easy	5
When you leave the bed you made	6
You can't lie there anymore,	7
Despite what everybody said.	8
And they're walking out the door	9
For the last time	10
And the sun comes shining through	11
And they'll never be alone	12
Walking home.	13
	14

End of question paper

PAPER C

QUESTION 1

This question features instrumental music.

Listen to this excerpt and identify **three** concepts in the music from those listed below.

Read through the concepts before hearing the music.

Baroque	Whole-tone scale
Harmonics	Sequence
Plagal cadence	Through-composed
Diminished 7th	Pedal
Symphony	

Insert your **three answers** on the lines below. 3

_____

_____

_____

The music will be played **twice** with a pause of 10 seconds between playings and a pause of 30 seconds before the next question starts.

Here is the music for the first time.
Here is the music for the second time.

QUESTION 2

In this question you will hear three male vocalists accompanied by orchestra.

A guide to the music is shown below. You are required to complete this guide by inserting music concepts.

There will now be a pause of 30 seconds to allow you to read through the question.

The music will be played three times with a pause of 10 seconds between playings. You will then have a further 20 seconds to complete your answer.

In the first two playings a voice will help guide you through the music. There is no voice in the third playing.

Here is the music for the first time.
Here is the music for the second time.
Here is the music for the third time.

---

1. The male vocalist is a/an

   _____   1

2. The time signature is

   _____   1

3. The melody is based on the

   _____ scale   1

4. The harmonic feature here is

   _____   1

5. The cadence is

   _____   1

QUESTION 3

This question features contrasting music for voices.

(a) Listen to this excerpt and insert the concept which describes (i) the style of the vocal composition and (ii) the style of soprano singing.

    (i)   Style of the vocal composition

           _____

           1

    (ii)   Style of soprano singing

           _____

           1

(b) Listen to a different excerpt and identify the type of chord at the end.

_____

           1

QUESTION 4

This question is based on a song from a musical.

Listen to the song and follow the guide to the music on the next page.

Here is the music for the first time.

You now have 2 minutes to read through the question.

All the answers must be written where marked on the next page.

(a) Insert the correct <u>time signature</u> in **bar 1** 1

(b) Write the name of the <u>interval</u> in **bar 10** 1

(c) Write the name of the <u>key</u> the music has modulated into in **bar 17**. 1

(d) Add <u>rests</u> to **bar 20** to make it correct. 1

(e) Transpose the music down 1 octave into the bass clef in **bars 26 and 27** There is no need to insert a key signature. 1

(f) Add <u>notes</u> to **bar 29** to match what you hear. The correct rhythm is written above. 1

Complete your answers during the next 3 playings.

The music will be played a further 3 times with a break of 30 seconds between playings.

Here is the music for the second time.
Here is the music for the third time.
Here is the music for the fourth time.

PAPER C

QUESTION 5

(a) Listen to this excerpt and tick **one** box to identify the scale this melody is based on.

☐ Major

☐ Minor

☐ Modal

☐ Pentatonic

1

Here is the music for the first time.
Here is the music for the second time.

(b) The melodic feature played by the saxophones and horns in this section is a/an

_____

1

(c) Listen to a different excerpt. Insert the concept which describes the type of group playing.

_____

1

30

Additional space for notes

(Turn over for Question 6)

QUESTION 6

This question is based on instrumental music.

In this question you should identify the most prominent concepts in the music.
As you listen, identify at least **two** concepts from each of the following headings:

Melody/Harmony   **Rhythm**   **Timbre**

You will hear the music **three times** and you should make notes as you listen.

Rough work will not be marked.

Marks will only be awarded for the final answer.

After the third playing you will have 3 minutes to write your final answer in the space provided.

Here is the music for the first time.
Here is the music for the second time.
Here is the music for the third time.   **6**

Rough Work

Melody/Harmony	
Rhythm	
Timbre	

Final Answer

PAPER C

QUESTION 7

This question features vocal music.

Listen to this excerpt and identify **four** concepts in the music from those listed below.

Read through the list before hearing the music.

Minor tonality	Oratorio
Contrapuntal	Lied
Recitative	A cappella
Homophonic	Discord
Plagal cadence	Syllabic

Insert your four answers on the lines below.   **4**

_____

_____

_____

_____

The music will be played **three** times with a pause of 10 seconds between playings and a pause of 40 seconds before the next question starts.

Here is the music for the first time.
Here is the music for the second time.
Here is the music for the third time.

QUESTION 8

This question is about comparing two excerpts of music.

Identify concepts present in each excerpt and then decide which **five** concepts are common to both excerpts. Both excerpts will be played **three** times with a pause of 10 seconds between playings.

As you listen, tick boxes in **Column A** and **Column B** to identify what you hear in Excerpt 1 and Excerpt 2.

These columns are for rough work only and will not be marked.

After the **three** playings of the music you will be given 2 minutes to decide which concepts are common to both excerpts and to tick **five** boxes in **Column C.**

PAPER C

You now have 1 minute to read through the question.

Here is Excerpt 1 for the first time. **Remember to tick concepts in Column A.**
Here is Excerpt 2 for the first time. **Remember to tick concepts in Column B.**

Here is Excerpt 1 for the second time.
Here is Excerpt 2 for the second time.

Here is Excerpt 1 for the third time.
Here is Excerpt 2 for the third time.

You now have two minutes to identify the **five** concepts common to both excerpts.

Remember to tick five boxes only in Column C.   5

	Concepts	Column A Excerpt 1	Column B Excerpt 2	Column C 5 features common to both
Styles	Concerto			
	Chamber Music			
	Minimalist			
Melody/Harmony	Trill			
	Chromatic scale			
	Melody played in octaves			
	Imperfect cadence			
Rhythm	Diminution			
	Triple time			
	Syncopation			
Structure/Form	Binary			
	Ternary			
	Sonata form			
	Strophic			

QUESTION 9

This question is based on a song from a musical.

Below is a list of features which you will hear in the music.

There will now be a pause of 1 minute to allow you to read through the question.

The lyrics of the song are printed on the next page. You should insert each feature you hear once in the right hand column at the point it occurs.
You need only write the underlined word.

- Clarinet ascending **arpeggio**

- **Off the beat** accompaniment begins

- **Recitative** type style

- **Dominant 7th** accented chords

- **Start of pizzicato** strings

The music will now be played three times with a pause of 20 seconds between playings, and a pause of 30 secs at the end.

Here is the music for the first time.
Here is the music for the second time.
Here is the music for the third time.

- Clarinet ascending **arpeggio**

- **Off the beat** accompaniment begins

- **Recitative** style

- **Dominant 7**[th] accented chords

- **Start of pizzicato** strings

Home of that new age jazz - Swing	1
Rock and Roll to the beat, beat, beat	2
Of Stevie Valency	3
And his crazy cats.	4
(Hey cats, getting over the square)	5
Swing! Dig the rhythm	6
Swing! Dig the message.	7
The jive is jumpin'	8
And the music goes round and round.	9
Whoa-ho, while you run around	10
Cats make it solid,	11
Cats make it groovy.	12
You gotta get your seafood, Mama	13
Your favourite dish is fish.	14
It's your favourite dish	15
Don't be square	16
Rock right out of that rocking chair.	17
Truck on down and let down your hair.	18
Breathe that barrel-house air	19
The village vortex.	20

End of Question Paper

PAPER D

QUESTION 1

This question features instrumental music.
Listen to this excerpt and identify **three** concepts in the music from those listed below.

Read through the concepts before hearing the music.

Plagal cadence	Harmonics
Through-composed	Syncopation
Mordent	Harmonic minor scale
Obbligato	Glissando
Brass band	

Insert your **three answers** on the lines below. **3**

_____

_____

_____

The music will be played **twice** with a pause of 10 seconds between playings and a pause of 30 seconds before the next question starts.

Here is the music for the first time.
Here is the music for the second time.

QUESTION 2

In this question you will hear a piece of film music.

A guide to the music is shown below. You are required to complete this guide by inserting music concepts.

There will now be a pause of 30 seconds to allow you to read through the question.

The music will be played three times with a pause of 20 seconds between playings. You will then have a further 30 seconds to complete your answer.

In the first two playings a voice will help guide you through the music. There is no voice in the third playing.

Here is the music for the first time.
Here is the music for the second time.
Here is the music for the third time.

1. The time signature is

   _____ 1

2. The French horns are playing a/an

   _____ 1

3. The harmonic device here is a/an

   _____ 1

4. The descending scale in the strings is

   _____ 1

5. The rhythmic feature here is

   _____ 1

QUESTION 3

This question features music for voices.

(a) Listen to this excerpt and (i) identify the final cadence and (ii) write the concept which describes unaccompanied singing.

   (i) The final cadence is

   _____
   1

   (ii) The concept to describe unaccompanied singing is

   _____
   1

(b) Listen to another excerpt and identify the descending scale sung by the basses. The extract will be played twice.

   _____
   1

Here is the music for the first time.
Here is the music for the second time.

PAPER D

QUESTION 4

This question is based on a jazz piano piece.

Listen to the music and follow the melody on the following page.

Here is the music for the first time.

You now have 2 minutes to read through the question.

All the answers must be written where marked in the music on the next page.

(a) Write the interval name in the box provided in **bar 1**.   **1**

(b) Write the names of the chords in the boxes at **bar 6 and bar 7**. The first chord is given. Choose either chord names (eg. **G**) or roman numerals (eg **I**)   **1**
from below

G	Chord I
C	Chord IV
D	Chord V
Em	Chord VI

(c) Add an accidental in **bar 7** to match what you hear.   **1**

(d) Write the correct notes in bar 8 to match what you hear. The correct rhythm is written above.   **1**

(e) Correct the rhythm of the notes under the bracket in **bar 10** to match what you hear.   **1**

(f) Add a symbol to show that the last note in **bar 11** is accented.   **1**

Complete your answers during the next 3 playings

The music will be played a further 3 times with a break of 30 seconds between playings.

Here is the music for the second time.

Here is the music for the third time.

Here is the music for the fourth time.

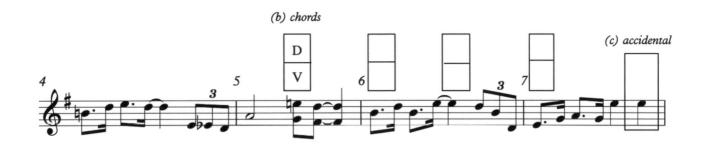
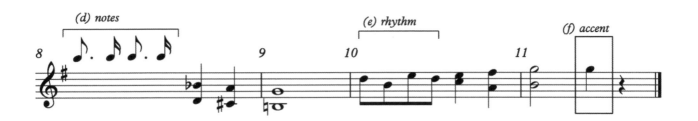

QUESTION 5

This question features an instrumental composition.

(a) Listen to the excerpt and tick **one** box which best describes the rhythmic feature.

☐ Irregular time signatures

☐ Augmentation

☐ Triplets

☐ Diminution

Here is the music for the first time.
Here is the music for the second time.

(b) Listen to the following excerpt and insert the name of the ornament you hear.

_____
                                                                        1

(c) Listen to a further excerpt and describe the playing technique of the guitar towards the end of the excerpt.

_____
                                                                        1

PAPER D

Additional space for notes

(Turn over for Question 6)

PAPER D

QUESTION 6

This question is based on instrumental music.

In this question you should identify the most prominent concepts in the music.
As you listen, identify at least **two** concepts from each of the following headings:

Harmony   **Rhythm/Form**   **Timbre**

You will hear the music **three times** and you should make notes as you listen.

Rough work will not be marked.

Marks will only be awarded for the final answer.

After the third playing you will have 3 minutes to write your final answer in the space provided.

Here is the music for the first time.
Here is the music for the second time.
Here is the music for the third time.   **6**

Rough Work

Harmony	
Rhythm/Form	
Timbre	

Final Answer

PAPER D

QUESTION 7

This question features vocal music.

Listen to this excerpt and identify **four** concepts in the music from those listed below.

Read through the list before hearing the music.

Lied	Jazz funk
Inverted pedal	Augmentation
Tierce de picardie	Compound time
Octave leap	Diminished 7th
Relative major	Da capo aria

Insert your **four** answers on the lines below.   4

_____

_____

_____

_____

The music will be played **three** times with a pause of 10 seconds between playings and a pause of 40 seconds before the next question starts.

Here is the music for the first time.
Here is the music for the second time.
Here is the music for the third time.

Additional space for notes

(Turn over for Question 8)

PAPER D

QUESTION 8

This question is about comparing two excerpts of music.

Identify concepts present in each excerpt and then decide which **five** concepts are common to both excerpts. Both excerpts will be played **three** times with a pause of 10 seconds between playings.

As you listen, tick boxes in **Column A** and **Column B** to identify what you hear in Excerpt 1 and Excerpt 2.
These columns are for rough work only and will not be marked.

After the **three** playings of the music you will be given 2 minutes to decide which concepts are common to both excerpts and to tick **five** boxes in **Column C**.
You now have 1 minute to read through the question.

Here is Excerpt 1 for the first time. **Remember to tick concepts in Column A.**
Here is Excerpt 2 for the first time. **Remember to tick concepts in Column B.**

Here is Excerpt 1 for the second time.
Here is Excerpt 2 for the second time.

Here is Excerpt 1 for the third time.
Here is Excerpt 2 for the third time.

You now have two minutes to identify the **five** concepts common to both excerpts.
Remember to tick five boxes only in Column C.

5

	Concepts	Column A Excerpt 1	Column B Excerpt 2	Column C 5 features common to both
Styles	Jazz			
	Sonata			
	Baroque			
	Impressionism			
Melody/Harmony	Trill			
	Acciacatura			
	Whole tone scale			
	Imperfect cadence			
Rhythm	Rallentando			
	3 against 2			
	Anacrusis			
Structure/Form	Tremolo			
	Contrary motion			
	Ritornello			

PAPER D

QUESTION 9

This question is based on a song from a musical.
Below is a list of features which you will hear in the music.

There will now be a pause of 1 minute to allow you to read through the question.

The lyrics of the song are printed on the next page. You should insert each feature you hear once in the right column at the point it occurs. You need only write the underlined word.

- **Ostinato** in accompaniment

- Descending **major scale** in accompaniment

- **Modulation** to new key

- **Dominant 7th** in vocal part

- **Imitation** in horn part

The music will now be played three times with a pause of 20 seconds between playings, and a pause of 30 secs at the end.

Here is the music for the first time.
Here is the music for the second time.
Here is the music for the third time.

Insert 5 concepts underlined where they appear. Write them once only in the right hand column.

- **Ostinato** in accompaniment
- Descending **major scale** in accompaniment
- **Modulation** to new key
- **Dominant 7th** in vocal part
- **Imitation** in horn part

A life with others	1
	2
Hand in hand.	3
	4
One day	5
	6
Our hearts will beat again.	7
	8
We'll live our lives	9
	10
As good and peaceful men	11
	12
Voices heard, our faces seen	13
	14
A nation guided	15
	16
By a dream.	17

End of question paper

PAPER E

QUESTION 1

This question features instrumental music.
Listen to this excerpt and identify **three** concepts in the music from those listed below.

Read through the concepts before hearing the music.

Interrupted cadence	Obbligato
Through-composed	Irregular time signatures
Triplets	Middle 8
Walking bass	Soul
Ripieno	

Insert your **three answers** on the lines below.   3

_____

_____

_____

The music will be played **twice** with a pause of 10 seconds between playings and a pause of 30 seconds before the next question starts.

Here is the music for the first time.
Here is the music for the second time.

QUESTION 2

In this question you will hear a Slow Air.

A guide to the music is shown below. You are required to complete this guide by inserting music concepts.

There will now be a pause of 30 seconds to allow you to read through the question.

The music will be played three times with a pause of 20 seconds between playings. You will then have a further 30 seconds to complete your answer.

In the first two playings a voice will help guide you through the music.

Here is the music for the first time.
Here is the music for the second time.
Here is the music for the third time.

PAPER E

Here is the music for the third time.

1. The music starts with a/an _____	1
2. The type of group playing is a/an _____	1
3. The Scottish influenced rhythm is a/an _____	1
4. The ornament is a/an _____	1
5. The music has modulated to the _____	1

QUESTION 3

This question features contrasting music for voices.

(a) Listen to this excerpt and insert the concept which describes the style of the music.

_____

1

(b) Listen to a different excerpt and insert the concept which describes the work this music is from.

_____

1

(c) Listen to a different part of the same music and identify the final cadence.

_____

1

PAPER E

QUESTION 4

Marks

This question is based on an arrangement of an orchestral piece.

Listen to the music and follow the guide on the next page.

Here is the music for the first time.

You now have 2 minutes read the questions.

All the answers must be written in the boxes on the next page.

(a) Insert a suitable tempo above **bar 1** from the list given.
      Lento   Adagio   Andante   Allegro   Presto   1

(b) Write the interval formed by the first and last notes bracketed in **bars 3 and 4.**

(c) Insert the names of the missing chords in **bars 7 & 8**. The first chord has been given.   1

Choose either the chord name (eg; F) or the chord position (eg; chord I)

F   Chord I
Bb   Chord IV
C   Chord V
Dm   Chord VI

Insert your answers in the boxes provided.

(d) Insert the missing notes in **bars 9 & 10**. The correct rhythm is written above the music.   1

(e) Correct the rhythm of the notes in **bar 11** to match what you hear.   1

(f) Name the cadence in **bars 13 &14**.   1

The music will be played 3 more times with a pause of 30 seconds between playings.

Here is the music for the second time
Here is the music for the third time
Here is the music for the fourth time

PAPER E

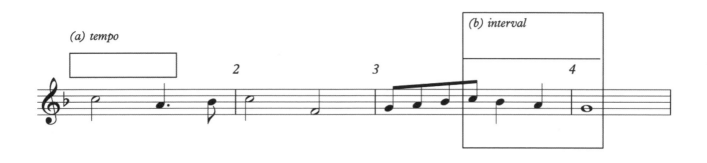
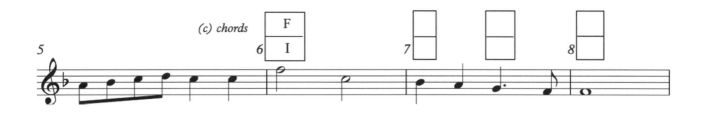
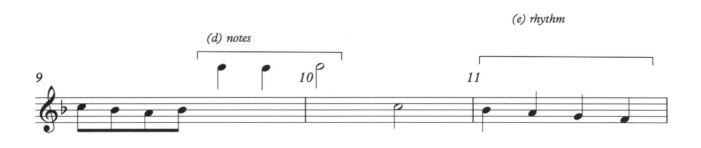
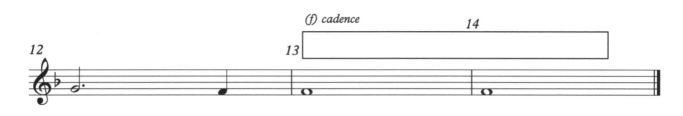

PAPER E

QUESTION 5

This question features instrumental music.

(a) Listen to this excerpt and tick **one** box to describe the structural feature.

   Here is the music for the first and only time.

   ☐ Through composed

   ☐ Polyphonic

   ☐ Sonata form

   ☐ Ritornello

   1

(b) Listen to this excerpt from the same piece and

   (i) insert the concept which describes the rhythmic feature present and
   (ii) identify the type of group playing

   (i) Rhythmic feature_____ **1**

   (ii) The type of group playing._____ **1**

   This excerpt is short and will be played twice.

   Here is the music for the first time.
   Here is the music for the second time

Additional space for notes

(Turn over for Question 6)

PAPER E

QUESTION 6

This question is based on instrumental music.

In this question you should identify the most prominent concepts in the music.
As you listen, identify at least **two** concepts from each of the following headings:

Melody/Harmony   **Rhythm**   **Timbre/Dynamics**

You will hear the music **three times** and you should make notes as you listen.

Rough work will not be marked.

Marks will only be awarded for the final answer.
After the third playing you will have 3 minutes to write your final answer in the space provided.

Here is the music for the first time.
Here is the music for the second time.
Here is the music for the third time.   **6**

Rough Work

Melody/Harmony	
Rhythm	
Timbre/Dynamics	

Final Answer

_____

_____

_____

_____

_____

_____

_____

_____

QUESTION 7

This question features vocal music.
Listen to this excerpt and identify **four** concepts in the music from those listed below.

Read through the list before hearing the music.

Coloratura	Time changes
Pedal	Concertino
Time changes	Lied
Plainchant	Diminished 7th
Perfect cadence	Da capo aria

Insert your four answers on the lines below.   4

The music will be played **three** times with a pause of 10 seconds between playings and a pause of 40 seconds before the next question starts.

_____

_____

_____

Here is the music for the first time.
Here is the music for the second time.
Here is the music for the third time.

PAPER E

QUESTION 8

This question is about comparing two excerpts of music.

Identify concepts present in each excerpt and then decide which **five** concepts are common to both excerpts. Both excerpts will be played **three** times with a pause of 10 seconds between playings.

As you listen, tick boxes in **Column A** and **Column B** to identify what you hear in Excerpt 1 and Excerpt 2.

These columns are for rough work only and will not be marked.

After the **three** playings of the music you will be given 2 minutes to decide which concepts are common to both excerpts and to tick **five** boxes in **Column C**.

You now have 1 minute to read through the question.

Here is Excerpt 1 for the first time. **Remember to tick concepts in Column A.**
Here is Excerpt 2 for the first time. **Remember to tick concepts in Column B.**

Here is Excerpt 1 for the second time.
Here is Excerpt 2 for the second time.

Here is Excerpt 1 for the third time.
Here is Excerpt 2 for the third time.

You now have two minutes to identify the **five** concepts common to both excerpts.

Remember to tick five boxes only in Column C.

	Concepts	Column A Excerpt 1	Column B Excerpt 2	Column C 5 features common to both
Styles	Oratorio			
	Impressionism			
	Sonata			
	20th century			
Melody/Harmony	Imitation			
	Trills			
	Acciaccatura			
	Atonal			
Rhythm	Diminution			
	Compound time			
	Accelerando			
Structure/Form	Homophonic			
	Musique concrete			
	Polyphonic			

QUESTION 9

This question is based on an arrangement of a Scottish song.

Below is a list of features which occur in the music.

There will now be a pause of 1 minute to allow you to read through the question.

The lyrics of the song are printed in the table on the opposite page. You should insert each feature **once** in the column on the right at the point where it occurs.

You need only insert the underlined word.
- Descending **scale** sung in thirds
- First instance of an **octave** interval in the voice
- **Tremolando** in the strings
- **Perfect** cadence
- **Pedal**

The music will now be played **three** times with a pause of 20 seconds between playings and a pause of 30 seconds at the end.

Here is the music for the first time.
Here is the music for the second time.
Here is the music for the third time.

- Descending **scale** sung in thirds
- First instance of an **ascending octave** interval in the voice
- **Tremolando** in the strings
- **Perfect** cadence
- **Pedal**

Insert the **five** underlined words at the point they occur.

Insert each word once only.   **5**

Instrumental introduction	1
O gem of the Hebrides	2
Bathed in the light.	3
Of the midsummer dawning	4
That follows the night.	5
How I yearn for the cries	6
Of the seagulls in flight.	7
As they circle high above	8
The Dark Island.	9
Oh, isle of my childhood	10
I'm dreaming of thee.	11
As the steamer leaves Oban	12
And passes Tiree.	13
Soon I'll capture the magic	14
That lingers for me.	15
When I'm back once more upon	16
The Dark Island.	17
When I'm back once more upon	18
The Dark Island.	19

End of question paper